discovermore

Earth Science

The Rock Cycle

Theia Lake

Britannica Educational Publishing
IN ASSOCIATION WITH
THE ROSEN PUBLISHING GROUP

Published in 2026 by Britannica Educational Publishing (a trademark of Encyclopædia Britannica, Inc.) in association with The Rosen Publishing Group, Inc.
2544 Clinton Street, Buffalo, NY 14224

Distributed exclusively by Rosen Publishing.
To see additional Britannica Educational Publishing titles, go to rosenpublishing.com.

Editor: Danielle Haynes
Book Design: Michael Flynn

Photo Credits: Cover Shutterstock.com; (series background) Dai Yim/Shutterstock.com; p. 4 maxpro/Shutterstock.com; p. 5 LarysaPol/Shutterstock.com; p. 6 yusufdemirci/Shutterstock.com; p. 7 www.sandatlas.org/Shutterstock.com; p. 8 Saint Images/Shutterstock.com; p. 9 Yes058 Montree Nanta/Shutterstock.com; p. 10 Robert Crow/Shutterstock.com; p. 11 Zephyr_p/Shutterstock.com; p. 12 Nastya22/Shutterstock.com; p. 13 NickKnight/Shutterstock.com; p. 14 Jane_MM/Shutterstock.com; p. 15 Mark Brandon/Shutterstock.com; p. 16 MDSPhotos/Shutterstock.com; p. 17 stihii/Shutterstock.com; p. 18 anindyaestiandari/Shutterstock.com; p. 19 Walter Bilotta/Shutterstock.com; p. 20 LesPalenik/Shutterstock.com; p. 21 Nenad Cavoski/Shutterstock.com; p. 22 H.R. Photos/Shutterstock.com; p. 23 NairaCapture/Shutterstock.com; p. 25 (top) Arlene Waller/Shutterstock.com; p. 25 (bottom) steflas/Shutterstock.com; p. 26 Kaentian Street/Shutterstock.com; p. 27 Rita Meraki/Shutterstock.com; p. 28 Marinodenisenko/Shutterstock.com; p. 29 VectorMine/Shutterstock.com.

Cataloging-in-Publication Data

Names: Lake, Theia.
Title: The rock cycle / Theia Lake.
Description: New York : Britannica Educational Publishing, in association with Rosen Educational Services, 2026. | Series: Discover more: earth science | Includes glossary and index.
Identifiers: ISBN 9781641904285 (library bound) | ISBN 9781641904278 (pbk) | ISBN 9781641904292 (ebook)
Subjects: LCSH: Geochemical cycles--Juvenile literature.
Classification: LCC Q180.2 L35 2026 | DDC 551.9--dc23

Manufactured in the United States of America

CPSIA Compliance Information: Batch #CSBRIT26. For further information contact Rosen Publishing at 1-800-237-9932.

Contents

Rocks of All Shapes and Sizes

Most of the Earth's surface is made up of rocks of different types. There's rock under your feet even if you can't see it—even under the oceans! We see rocks around us every day. Rocks are in the walls of buildings, in the ground we walk on, and in the pebbles and cliffs at the beach. There are rocks under the sea and in the soil. Rocks make the landscapes we see around us.

Cliffs and mountains are mostly made up of rock.

You can find examples of different rocks all in the same spot, such as on a riverbed or seashore.

There are many different types of rocks in the world. Rocks can be as small as a grain of sand or as big as a building. Some rocks are hard, but some are soft and crumbly. Rocks come in different colors, too, from pink, white, and silver to gray and black. Rocks are made from one or many **minerals**. Each has their own qualities and appearance.

WORD WISE

MINERALS ARE THE SOLID PARTS THAT MAKE UP ROCKS.

The Layers of Earth

Most minerals form deep inside the very center of the Earth in a layer called the core. Above the core, the center part of Earth, is a thick layer of extremely hot rock called the mantle. Earth's hard, rocky outer layer is called the crust. When rock deep in Earth's crust or the mantle melts, we call it magma. As magma flows upward, it cools. As it cools, different materials inside it harden and become tiny solid minerals that can form rocks.

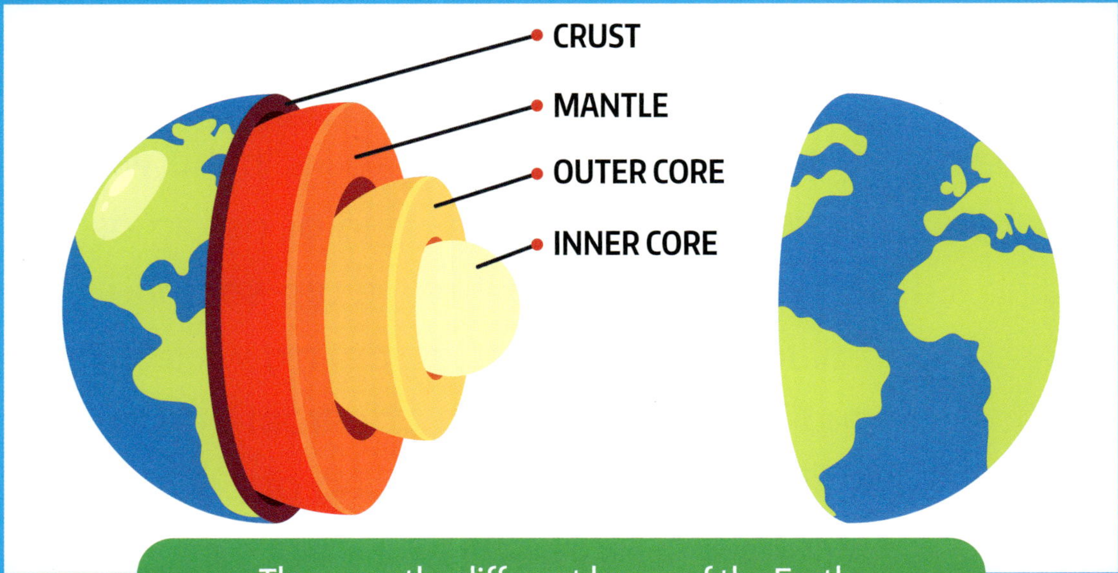

These are the different layers of the Earth.
The outer crust is much thinner than the inside layers.

The mineral peridotite forms deep in the Earth's mantle.

Some minerals form when water gets under Earth's surface. Rain and seawater seep underground through cracks in the crust. Some of this water heats up if it reaches the hot mantle rock. Minerals in the very hot water mix with minerals from the mantle rock. When the water cools again, new minerals form. The most common minerals found in the mantle are olivine, garnet, and pyroxene.

Consider This

When rocks heat up, they change. How do we use heat to change things? How does heat change ice cream on a summer's day?

The Rock Cycle

Rocks and minerals are ever changing. They are always changing because they are always being recycled. Rocks are formed, worn down, and then formed again in a process called the rock cycle. The **rock cycle** keeps recycling the minerals in Earth's crust.

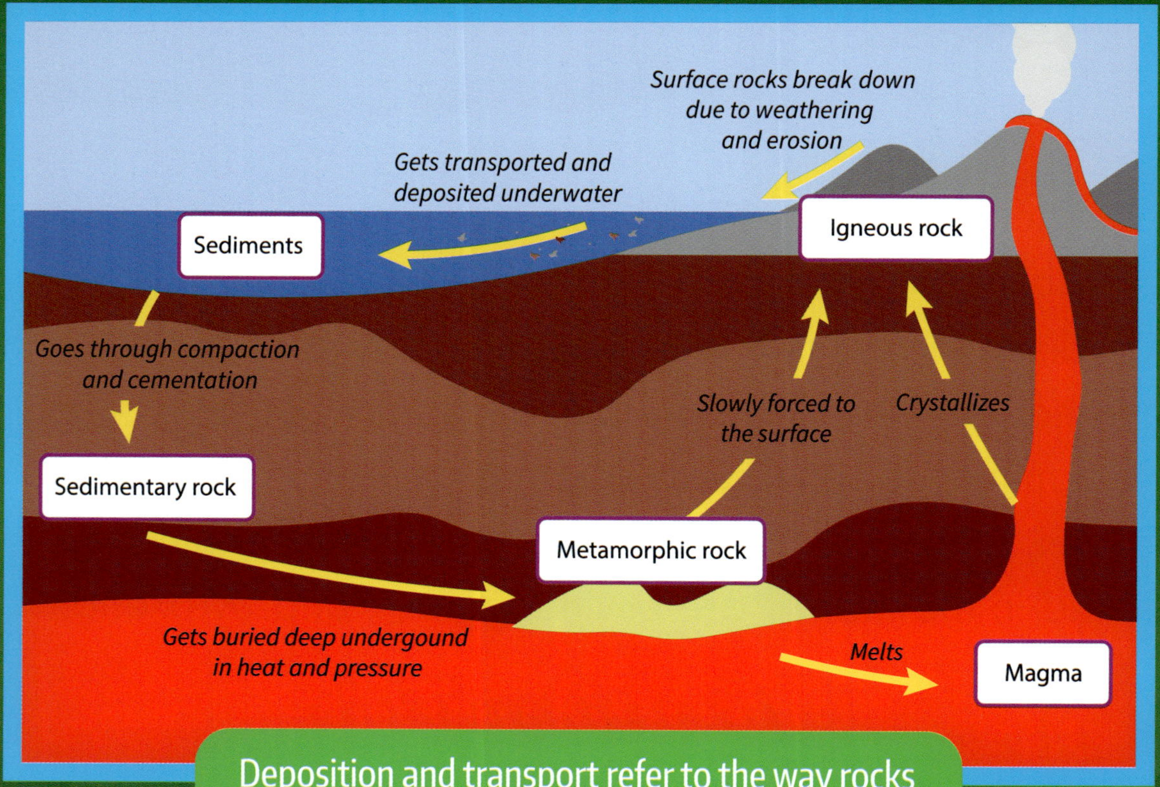

Deposition and transport refer to the way rocks are moved from one location to another.

About 70 percent of all sedimentary rocks in Earth's crust are shale. Shale is flat and splits into thin, parallel layers.

Rocks can be divided into three main types: igneous, sedimentary, and metamorphic. The types of rock are defined by how they are formed in the rock cycle. Igneous and metamorphic rocks are the most common rock types in Earth's crust. Sedimentary rock is the most common rock type exposed at its surface.

WORD WISE

THE ROCK CYCLE IS THE PROCESS BY WHICH ROCKS OF ONE KIND CHANGE INTO ROCKS OF ANOTHER KIND. THE ROCK CYCLE TAKES MANY MILLIONS OF YEARS.

Igneous Rocks

Igneous rocks are the most common type of rocks found in the Earth's crust. Igneous rocks form from hot magma that escapes from deep inside Earth. Earth's crust may seem solid and very strong, but there are places where it is weak. At these points, magma can sometimes build up and suddenly burst through the crust. This is what happens when volcanoes erupt.

As lava cools during a volcanic eruption, it forms new igneous rock.

Granite is very popular for its use in kitchen countertops because it's strong.

When magma escapes onto Earth's surface, we call it lava. In the cool air above ground, the red-hot lava starts to quickly cool down. As it cools, it gets harder and becomes rock. The exact type of rock that forms depends on what minerals were in the magma, but two common igneous rocks are granite and basalt. These two types of rocks are useful in building and paving.

Consider This

Some volcanoes erupt at the very bottom of an ocean. Could this explain how some islands form?

Clear as Crystals

Sometimes, rocks contain special surprises! Crystals can form when the magma from inside Earth cools and hardens into rock. Crystals are made of minerals that have formed into shapes. These solid pieces of rock have flat sides and sharp, clear edges and corners. Minerals do not become crystal shapes if they form rock in spaces where there is not enough room to do so.

Quartz is the most common crystal on Earth, but it can have many different colors and shapes.

Alexandrite is one of the most rare crystals on Earth. It appears green in natural sunlight and red in incandescent light.

Some crystals are very small, such as those that you find inside pieces of granite. Other crystals can be huge. Crystals are small if rock cools quickly. They are large if lava cools slowly into rock. Some crystals are dull, and others are shiny or colorful. Some, such as alexandrite, can even appear to change colors.

Consider This

Why do you think crystals such as diamonds and sapphires are worth far more than quartz crystals, which make up most of the sand found on a beach?

Sedimentary Rocks

Of all the rocks exposed on Earth's surface, you're most likely to come across sedimentary. Sedimentary rock can be formed in several ways. Some is formed when rocks of any kind are worn away by wind, rain, and other elements. Through a process called erosion, tiny pieces of the original rock, along with dissolved minerals, are carried away to another site. Over time, millions of tiny pieces of **sediment** pile up on top of each other. Gradually, thick layers of sediment build up.

Sedimentary rock is most easily identified by the layers it creates.

Sometimes, animals and plants get trapped within layers of sediment. Over time, they become fossils embedded within the sedimentary rock.

As the layers of sediment build up, the upper layers press down on the lower layers, squeezing the water out of them. The heavy weight of the upper layers presses the lower layers of mud, sand, and rock closer and closer together. Slowly, the pieces form new sedimentary rock. This process takes millions of years!

WORD WISE

SEDIMENT IS A NATURALLY FORMED MATERIAL THAT IS MADE OF TINY PIECES OF ROCK, MUD, OR SAND.

Finding Fossils

Crystals aren't the only fun surprises you might find hidden in rocks, there are also fossils! Fossils are the remains of plants and animals that lived millions of years ago. Most fossils are of sea animals that had shells. When a sea animal died and sank to the sea floor, its body quickly rotted away. The shell that remained was gradually buried under many layers of sediment.

Trilobites were a type of sea animal that are now extinct. We know they existed because of the fossils they left behind.

The dinosaur dies in a river.

The body is covered with sediment.
The meat decomposes.
The dinosaur beomes a fossil.

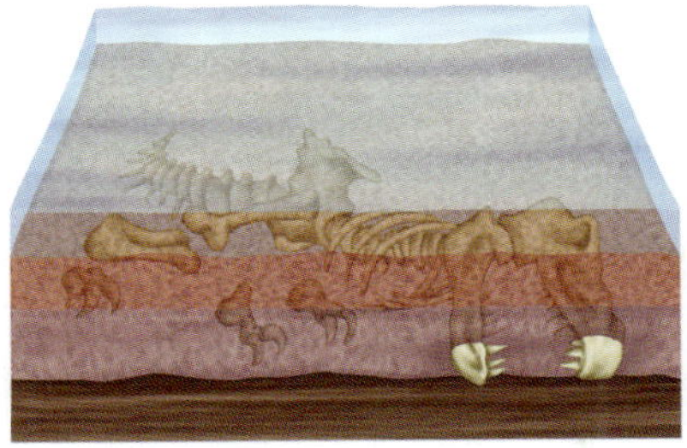

The sediments become rock.
The skeleton is pressed.

The earth's movements raise the layers of the rocks to the surface.

The rock erodes, exposing the fossil.

It takes millions of years for a fossil to form and then be exposed as part of the rock cycle.

Over hundreds of thousands of years, water carrying tiny pieces of sediment soaked into the shell. Gradually, minerals from the water replaced the minerals that made up the shell. The minerals turned into rock that was exactly the same shape as the shell, creating a fossil. Other kinds of fossils are imprints on soft material that later hardened into rock, such as dinosaur footprints in mud. Scientists have even found human fossils and footprints in rocks.

Consider This

Why do you think animals with shells were more likely to become fossils than other types of animals?

Metamorphic Rocks

The final type of rock is metamorphic. Metamorphic rock is formed when other rocks inside Earth are affected by great temperatures and pressures. There, it is extremely hot and the weight of the rock in the crust above presses down hard on the rock below. These conditions bake and break down minerals in the rock deep underground. When the minerals mix together again, they form new metamorphic rock. Metamorphic rock can be formed from sedimentary or igneous rocks.

Under a microscope, you can see how metamorphic rock is made up of millions of smaller crystals and rocks stuck together.

Marble is a type of metamorphic rock that people use for art, flooring, and countertops.

Metamorphic rock often forms in places where large sections of Earth's crust called plates push against each other. The rock can also form where magma is forced through existing rocks, heating them and increasing pressure, but not melting them like igneous rocks.

Consider This

Metamorphic rocks are not made by melting rocks. How does this differ from the way that igneous rocks are made?

Twisting Rock

Some metamorphic rocks have wiggly lines running through them. They are created when the crust moves slightly over the hot, bubbling mantle inside Earth. As the crust moves, the extreme heat and **pressure** from the rocks above twist and shape metamorphic rock as it forms.

Gneiss is an example of metamorphic rock. It looks a little like sedimentary rock because of the layers, but remember that metamorphic lines are more curved.

The ancient Romans were the first people to use slate for roofing material.

Slate is a metamorphic rock formed by extreme pressure underground. It is created by minerals that once made up a sedimentary rock called shale. The minerals that form slate are quite thin and flaky. Layers of slate break off easily into thin slabs. This is what makes slate such a useful material for making roof tiles. It's also been used for flooring and to make blackboards, writing tablets, and lab tabletops.

WORD WISE

PRESSURE IS A WEIGHT THAT PUSHES DOWN HEAVILY ON SOMETHING.

Weathering Away

Rocks may seem like the hardest, toughest substances on Earth. But even they don't last forever. All rocks on Earth's surface are affected by weathering. They are broken down into smaller pieces by the action of wind, water, and ice. When water gets into gaps in a rock and freezes into ice, it takes up more space. This makes the rock crack and break.

Here you can see how frozen water has gotten bigger and caused a rock to split apart.

The action of wind moving sand against rock formations in the U.S. Southwest creates these beautiful slot canyons.

On the coast, waves crash against the rocks and toss other rocks and stones at them. This breaks up rock. Rain can contain substances that **dissolve** rock and break it up. In sandy places, wind whips up many tiny pieces of sand and smashes them against rock. This action wears away the rock and creates more sand.

WORD WISE

DISSOLVING IS WHEN A SOLID BREAKS DOWN IN A LIQUID.

Erosion and Deposition

While some people may use the words "weathering" and "erosion" to mean the same thing, they're two different processes. Erosion is the movement of small pieces of rock broken up by weathering. Water, wind, and other natural forces cause rocks and earth to wear away, or erode. Erosion happens in different ways. Some broken pieces of rock simply drop to the ground and slip or roll down slopes. Others are carried off by rivers and streams. Wind picks up and carries small grains of sand. Glaciers are slow-moving rivers of ice, and they can shift or erode even big pieces of stone.

The tiny pieces of rock do not carry on moving. Eventually, the wind stops blowing, rivers flow into the sea, and glaciers melt. Then they drop the pieces of rock they were carrying. This process is called deposition. These tiny pieces of sand, mud, and pebbles gradually become buried and transformed into sedimentary rock. It's all part of the rock cycle.

Glaciers can break apart rocks in a process called weathering. It then moves those broken pieces along the path to a lake or the ocean, which is called erosion.

compareandcontrast

What are the similarities and differences between weathering, erosion, and deposition?

Weathering broke big and small pieces of rock apart on these rock formations. Erosion carried the pieces away, and the process of deposition left big boulders lying nearby.

The Importance of Soil

Did you know soil is made up of small rocks and other matter? Soil is an important part of the rock cycle. Plants grow in the top layer of soil. The waste in this layer contains nutrients. Without plants to eat or to feed the animals that provide people with meat, humans would not survive.

You can see here that soil builds up on top of rock in the ground. Plants then grow in the soil.

Soil can look and feel different depending on the types of rocks in it. Some soils have lots of clay, while others are more sandy.

Some of the main ingredients of soil are the tiny pieces of rock and sand formed by weathering and erosion. When plants start to grow among the bits of rock, they open up spaces between the pieces. Then, water, air, and animal or plant remains pass through the spaces. All these things combine to form what we call soil. Soil forms slowly. A layer of soil that is 1 inch (2.5 cm) thick may take 500 to 1,000 years to form. Over time, more and more soil builds up, compressing the layers of soil beneath into new sedimentary rock.

Consider This

Why do people try to stop the erosion of top layers of soil, for example, by building walls around a sloping field?

The Rock Cycle and People

Rocks are incredibly useful to people, and not just by providing the soil in which we grow our food. People cut rocks such as granite to make building materials. They use quartz from sand to make glass. Concrete is made from tiny pieces of rock and sand mixed with cement. Rock is mixed with tar to make the surface of streets.

The gas in our cars and most of the electricity we use to power machines such as computers come from fossil fuels. Coal, oil, and natural gas are fossil fuels. They formed from ancient plant and animal remains. The heavy weight of all the rock forming above the remains helped to turn them into the fuels we rely on today. It takes millions of years for these fossil fuels to be created.

People carved buildings directly into the rock in Petra, Jordan.

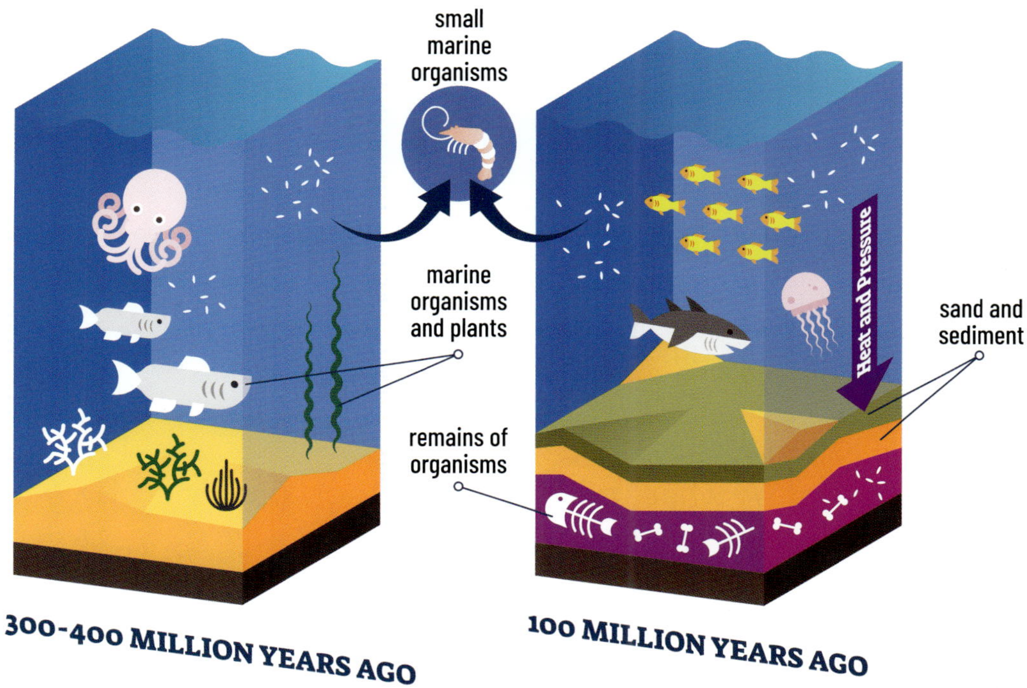

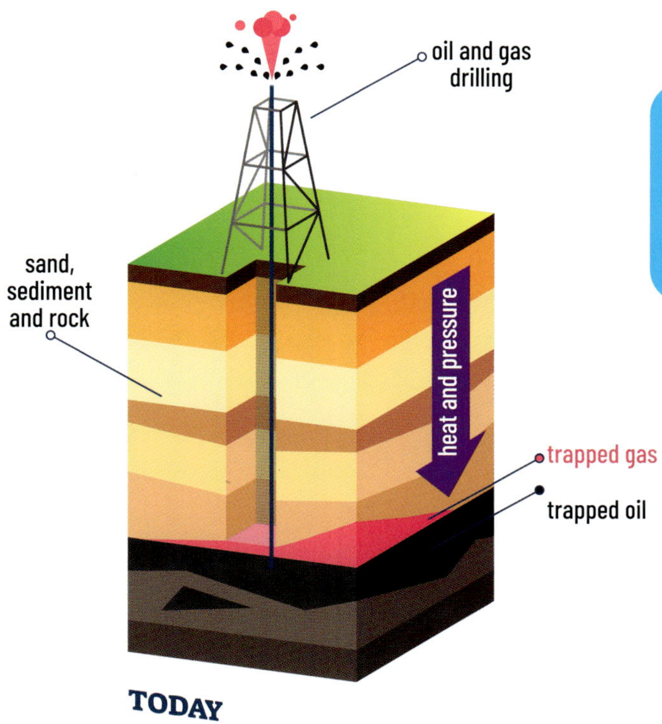

Consider This

We are using up Earth's supply of oil and gas very quickly. Why will there be no more when the supplies run out?

Time and pressure from layers of sand, sediment, and rock turn the remains of dead organisms into oil and gas.

Glossary

crumbly The quality of falling apart easily.

erupt The process by which a volcano sends hot, liquid rock and ash into the air.

expose To make known or visible.

extinct No longer existing.

incandescent A white, glowing light often produced by a particular kind of light bulb.

landscapes Natural features found on Earth's surface.

nutrients The substances that feed living things and help them live and grow.

parallel Objects that are side by side, running in the same direction.

pebble A very tiny rock.

process A series of actions that end in a particular result.

quality Characteristic.

seep To flow through small openings.

volcano An opening in Earth's surface where magma escapes from underground.

For More Information

Books

Gieseke, Tyler. *The Rock Cycle*. Minneapolis, MN: DiscoverRoo, 2023.

McDougal, Anna. *The Rock Cycle*. Buffalo, NY: Enslow Publishing, 2024.

Sauble, Audrey. *Can a Rock Grow?* Portland, OR: Larch Books, 2021.

Websites

Ducksters: Rocks
www.ducksters.com/science/rocks.php
Read more about the different types of rocks and the rock cycle.

Kiddle: Rock Cycle
www.kids.kiddle.co/Rock_cycle
Learn more about the processes on Earth that drive the rock cycle.

Index